THEN & NOW
with Terry Gorman

ald
Print

Printed and published by:
ALD Design & Print
279 Sharrow Vale Road
Sheffield S11 8ZF

Telephone 0114 267 9402
E:mail a.lofthouse@btinternet.com

ISBN 1-901587-64-9

Published June 2007

Terry Gorman

Perhaps it was the fact that I lived in close proximity to the city centre that I took such an early interest in Sheffield, its buildings and its people. As an eight-year-old restless, inquisitive but observant boy, I quickly discovered just about every back street, lane, alleyway, ramp and loading bay in town. Aided and abetted by Tony Rolley, my pal from around the corner in Charlotte Road, we would roam through the Norfolk Market Hall and the old Rag and Tag market, not forgetting Maces Pet and Feed shop, situated half below ground level in Exchange St., before taking the most roundabout and complicated route home.

All this had begun during the early war years of the 1940s, when many buildings had been destroyed, some left partly demolished but still able to carry on functioning, others re-locating to temporary premises until the war was over. Severe damage to my home had meant that we had to live away from Sheffield for some time, returning in 1943, when my familiarity with the city centre began. Riding on the upper deck of a tramcar through the town revealed a wealth of architectural detail not seen from ground level. This was to become the focus of my paintings in later years.

My education suffered in those war years. I was forced to move from school to school, sometimes being taught in groups of four or six in someone's front room, and finishing my school years at Sheffield Central Technical School, making a total of eight schools from start to finish. Unfortunately I failed the entrance exam to the Sheffield School of Art, then situated on Arundel Street. I had been sent into this exam by my school, armed with one 2H pencil, a synthetic rubber and a ruler. The first thing that I was expected to draw was a bucket, a scrubbing brush and a bar of carbolic soap on the enormous sheet of paper provided. I had never seen such a large sheet. I had been used to drawing on scraps and off-cuts of wallpaper. It was hopeless trying to shade with a 2H pencil. I couldn't fail to fail, and I did.

Leaving school in 1950 I became an apprentice plumber but, after only one day I, realised that this wasn't going to be my cup of tea, although I stuck at it until called up for National Service in the R.A.F., which was an

education in itself. Sheffield, by this time, was beginning to change; new road layouts, re-developments and modernisation were taking place, sometimes at the expense of some lovely old premises.

My next twenty-eight years or so were spent on the Sheffield City Ambulance Service, towards the end of which I had resurrected my interest in drawing and painting. Quite a few of my early paintings of the City and its surroundings were sold to the Philip Francis Gallery on Ecclesall Road. Interest in my work grew, which was quite fortunate as I had to retire from the Ambulance Service at the age of fifty, with a recurring injury.

I now needed to take painting seriously and work to become established in an area where there was strong competition from other artists painting in a similar style and with the same focus on Sheffield scenes. I quickly began to market my prints, selling the originals for ever increasing fees, which funded further prints for my portfolio. Helped along by family and friends, and by increasing sales at major outlets in Sheffield, I was able to use my childhood memories and experiences to re-create a series of atmospheric pictures of a Sheffield of the 1940s and 50s which have proved to be popular, not only here in the City, but in other parts of the country, and indeed the world, especially with those ex-Sheffielders now living overseas.

Many of us probably think of old Sheffield in black and white, as in the many collections of photographs, so I hope that this selection of paintings will bring some colour to the past, as seen through the eyes of Terry Gorman. I have attempted to capture the spirit, the character, the warmth and the humour of Sheffield and its people. I hope that I have succeeded.

Terry Gorman

London Road

A common sight on the streets until recent years was the rag and bone man who would take away old clothing, metal objects, and anything that was of no further use. His cry of "any old iron" would be heard several streets away. In exchange he would give a goldfish, a balloon or two, or a piece of donkey stone, used to whiten door steps. Boys would often be seen riding two or more to a bike, but would need to be on the look out for a "copper" or else!

Hillsborough Football Ground

The Sheffield Wednesday ground, a few minutes before the kick off in a Cup Tie, is featured here. The new Kop roof, now in place, keeps the fans protected in bad weather after years of being open to the elements. The North Stand on the right was built when the club hosted World Cup matches in 1966. The floodlight pylons have since been removed.

A few late comers are seen here making their way to the turnstiles on Penistone Road.

The Fair

It was only a short time after the end of the war that Pond Sreet was the venue for a spectacular fair, the first since the war began, and the first that I, as an 11 year old, had ever witnessed.

Unfortunately, it only lasted for a couple of weeks before moving on, but what an experience it had been. My favourite ride had been the Shamrock, with its loud hissing steam engine driven movement, quite scary at the time. The wonderful atmosphere was enjoyed by many.

The Sheffield Hallam University now occupies the site, which had for many years been a car park.

Button Lane

The well known Angel Inn was situated at the end of Button Lane which ran from the Moorhead, crossing Carver Street and Rockingham Street. There was always a fruit barrow standing at the end and a row of small shops which included a pork shop, a tailoring shop and a theatrical supplies shop. Apparently elephants were once stabled under the archway of the Angel Inn between performances at the Empire Theatre.

The back corner of Debenhams's store now occupies this site.

BUTTON LANE

The Moorhead at Christmas

This painting holds a special significance for me, as this is how Redgates Toy Shop looked before being destroyed by incendiaries in the Sheffield Blitz of December 1940. As a six year old I had been taken to see Santa in his Grotto in the basement of the store the day before the raid. I had set my mind on the red pedal car seen in the painting. Of course I never got it and, for all I know, it could still be under the foundations of the buildings now occupying the site.

The Wicker Matinee

This painting shows the Wicker Arches from Spital Hill with the city centre forming the back-drop. Beneath the arches can be seen the Wicker Cinema, with patrons queuing for the afternoon matinee.

The usual flow of traffic between the city and Attercliffe is under way, with the billboards on Spital Hill advertising an Abbott and Costello comedy film, and the city football clubs' forthcoming fixtures, amongst others.

Town Hall Square

The delightful garden roundabout, with its water feature and rock garden, occupied the centre of Town Hall Square for many years before giving way to larger designs, including the Goodwin Fountain. In this view the queues are already forming for the matinee at the Gaumont Cinema, formerly the Regent, while Wilson Peck displays the latest television sets and gramophones. Taxis are waiting on the rank, which was situated in the centre of the road in Barkers Pool.

Sheaf Square

A birdseye view over Sheaf Square outside the Midland Station gives some idea of the level of activity before the area was redeveloped a few decades ago, and recently up-graded. The unusually designed transport enquiry office was the focal point when leaving the station, with buses for Manchester, Buxton, Chesterfield and the Hope Valley operating from the terminus on the left of the scene. The distant view of the city centre and the western suburbs illustrates the hilly nature of Sheffield.

Templeborough

This industrial scene, set in 1947, depicts the huge steelworks at Templeborough which occupied the site of the present Magna complex. The painting shows steelworkers arriving by tram from Sheffield and Rotherham, some discussing the afternoon's Cup replay results as they report for their shifts. The fourteen chimneys were a landmark in the Don valley for many years.

TEMPLEBOROUGH

Images of an Era

The distinctive orange/brown façade of the former Prudential Building looks out over the Peace Gardens and Pinstone Street. In this painting, set in the 1950s, trams would pull into a designated lay-by to pick up and set down passengers at the covered tram stops in Pinstone Street allowing other 'through' trams to pass in both directions. One of the shops beneath the Prudential Building was Hobbies, where countless boys obtained kits and balsa wood for their models. The alleyway on the right led out into Barkers Pool between the cinema and Dainties sweet shop.

Sheffield United Football Ground

The South Stand was built when cricket finally transferred away from Bramall Lane in the 1970s. The stand occupies the ground where many famous cricketers had played and the present car park was the site of the cricket pavilion. This view shows the ground as a match is about to commence, shortly after the stand was opened.

Norfolk Bridge

Norfolk Bridge carried the Midland Railway over the River Don and Attercliffe Road at its junction with Sutherland Street. The bridge was always recognisable by its prominent Ferodo Brake Linings sign, which could be spotted from as far away as Crookes. With so many steelworks in the vicinity, this tram stop became a main picking-up and dropping-off point for steelworkers at shift change-over times.

Haymarket

Arguably the most congested and busiest thoroughfare in Sheffield during the1950s and 60s was Haymarket. The popularity of its shops and close proximity to the markets were the main factors, as well as the large amount of traffic, mainly trams and buses, travelling to and from the east end of the city and to Rotherham via The Wicker. The Norfolk Market Hall is on the left, with Dixon Lane leading down to the Rag and Tag Market. Trams for Rotherham left from around the corner in Exchange Street.

Saturday Night Out

Most districts of the city had their local cinema and the Scala at the corner of Winter Street and Brook Hill was always a big attraction on a Saturday night. There would be two 'houses' on Saturday night at the Scala, the first house at 6pm and the second at 8.15pm. Queues would form well in advance of the show, as was the case throughout the city in those days.

Old Georgian houses, the Childrens' Hospital and the University building all feature in this 1950s scene.

An operator would manually change the tram points to direct cars to either Crookes or Walkley as he saw them approaching up Houndsfield Road.

Hippodrome

The Hippodrome originally opened as a variety theatre with a seating capacity of 2760, becoming a cinema in 1931. The cheapest seats were in the 'gods' and were simply wooden benches situated on the third tier. It cost six old pence to get in, often after queuing for quite some time. This painting set in the 1950s is reminiscent of a typical Saturday night out, with buskers and ever present roast chestnut barrow.

Oxley's Menswear relocated to Broomhill when redevelopment took place. The long established Stokes paint and varnish manufacturing company still operates from Little London Road.

Pinstone Street and St. Pauls

St. Pauls Church was demolished in the mid 1930s and was replaced by the Peace Gardens, which themselves have been re modelled and upgraded with water features in the last few years. All the other buildings seen in this pre-war scene are still intact. Amazingly they all escaped damage during the blitz, when much of The Moor, a hundred yards away, was destroyed.

PINSTONE ST & ST PAULS CHURCH 1934

Attercliffe

The junction of Attercliffe Road and Staniforth Road was regarded as the gateway to the township of Attercliffe. The John Banner store was the focus for shoppers, and the building is still used by smaller shops in much the same way as before. The Astoria Ballroom was a popular venue for teenagers in the 1950s and was situated over the shops of the Burton's building. Attercliffe also had the Palace Theatre, where many well known artistes of the time began their careers, before going on to greater things.

Telegraph and Star

The Telegraph and Star building, formerly Kemsley House, is still one of the most recognisable and impressive structures in the City, and has remained relatively unchanged over the years. A Building Society now occupies the lower front section of the premises. The junction of Fargate and High Street was always hectic as shown in this late afternoon scene around 1939.

Paradise Square

The carol service in Paradise Square, featured here, took place in 1947 with the Cathedral choir leading the singing. The Salvation Army band took part along with office workers and passers by joining in. This became an annual event for several years.

PARADISE SQUARE
c 1949

Football Special

The corner of Shoreham Street and John Street is the setting for this snowy Saturday illustration of fans for a match. Trams bearing 'Football Special' on their destination indicators would ferry fans up from Fitzalan Square. They are seen here making their way into the ground. Overnight snow had put the game in doubt, but fans had helped to clear the pitch during the morning to allow the game to take place.

The chip shop partly visible on the left still caters for fans on match days, as it has done since before the war.

The Lansdowne

Originally the Lansdowne Cinema, this unique building was to become the temporary wartime premises of Marks and Spencer, prior to being opened as the Locarno ballroom. It was later used for Bingo, and then a night club, but then fell into serious disrepair. The oriental pagoda tower is still in existence. Hopefully it can be incorporated into the new development taking place.

The Cathedral

Founded by the De Lovetot family in the reign of Henry 1, the Cathedral, formerly the old Parish Church, contains the tombs and monuments of famous people from Sheffield's history such as the Earls of Shrewsbury. Other familiar names recorded are the Jessops, the Gells, and the Lawsons. A Chapter House, song school and vestries were added to the building in the 1930s with extensions to the west end completed in 1966. The church yard was originally paved with gravestones. A taxi rank ran down Church Street by the boundary railings.

Fargate

Fargate was the main road artery linking The Moor with the Haymarket area until it was pedestrianised in the 1970s. A constant flow of trams always gave Fargate a lively atmosphere and brought shoppers right into the heart of the main shopping area. Today the pedestrianisation of the area and the diversion of much of the through traffic to outer roads has given this part of the city centre a very different feel.

FARGATE c. 1936

Cole's Corner

Cole Brother's shop was situated at the corner of Fargate and High Street. The corner was a very popular and well known meeting place for Sheffield people over the years and is still fondly remembered by many who met there. The canopy provided shelter from the elements and the railings proved to be a useful prop or even a seat during many a long wait for a boyfriend or girlfriend to arrive for a date. An added bonus was that there were four reliable clocks which were visible from the corner, namely; the Cathedral, Sheffield Goldsmiths, the Telegraph and Star, and the Town hall. Cole Brothers later relocated to a site in Barker's Pool.

Rag and Tag

The Broad Street entrance to the old Rag and Tag market was always thronged with shoppers, especially around Christmas time. Stalls selling mainly fruit and vegetables extended to the top of Dixon Lane. Castlefolds wholesale fruit and vegetable market occupied the site across from the Rag and Tag entrance and, with the close proximity of the Norfolk Market Hall, provided people with a wonderful variety of goods at cheap prices.

Market Day

The colours of the awnings in this view of the Rag and Tag market have been exaggerated to bring some brightness to what would have otherwise been a dull scene. Benson's carpets and Rugs, the Herbalist's stall, the ironmonger, the home made sweetshop and Edwards's Pot stall were major attractions for shoppers. Not to be missed was the lady with the brass weighing machine where, for a penny, you could be weighed sitting in a plush red velvet seat. Spot the artist and his pal with a goldfish in a jam jar, obtained from Maces Pet Shop in Exchange Street.

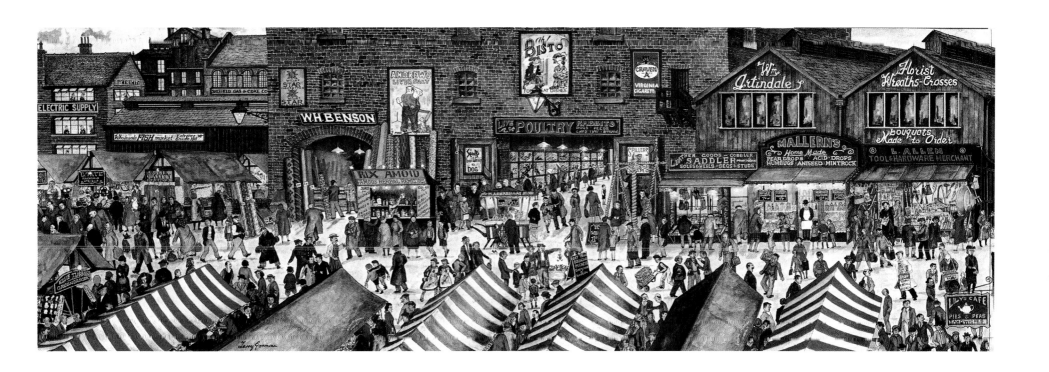

Fitzalan Square

A distant view of High Street can be seen from the bottom corner of Fitzalan Square. The Burton's building, C & A and the Marples Hotel were destroyed in the bombing of December 12th with huge loss of life. They were rebuilt following the end of the war. The Square acted as a terminus for trams for Wadsley Bridge, Owlerton and Darnall, as well as the many football specials to Bramall Lane and Hillsborough.

Wet & Wild

Bomb damage was still in evidence in much of the city centre well into the 1950s as can be seen here in Haymarket. Trams waiting to enter Fitzalan Square are seen with their passengers alighting into a typical November gloom, while a queue forms outside the temporary premises of Central Dairy Products in King Street in 1949.

Victoria Station

Victoria Station was closed when the Sheffield to Manchester railway line closed to passenger traffic in 1970. Countless Sheffield holidaymakers and fishermen have humped their luggage and fishing tackle up the station approach on their way to Cleethorpes and the River Trent. The hotel, now part of The Holiday Inn Group, is still operating successfully.

The Wicker Arches

The Wicker Arches were always regarded as the gateway to the city.   Passenger and freight rail traffic travelled over the arches on the L.N.E.R. rail line, which linked the eastern counties with Manchester in the west. The road passing beneath was the main road connecting Sheffield with Rotherham and Doncaster. The Royal Victoria Station was accessible by lift from the Wicker, fare one old penny, and is just visible on the right of the picture, though the main approach to the station was from Blonk Street.

The Lyceum and Theatre Royal

One of my first paintings was of the Lyceum theatre, with the Theatre Royal seen in the background. Before the days of television there would always be queues outside theatres and cinemas, and these in turn would attract buskers, entertainers and traders selling their wares as here, where a roast chestnut barrow is doing a good trade.

The view is from Arundel Street, opposite the stage door. The Theatre Royal was destroyed by fire in 1935. The Adelphi Hotel on the right is said to have been the venue for the formation of the Yorkshire County Cricket Club.

LYCEUM & THEATRE ROYAL c 1936

Moorhead

Robert Brothers, a well known store which survived well into the post war era, is seen here along with another famous landmark of the time, the Transport Department enquiry and information office. It looked rather like a filled in bandstand, overlooked by the Crimea Monument. On the right are the showrooms of the Newton Chambers Company, occupying a site at the junction of Furnival Street and Union Street. Set in the mid 1930s and painted in 1986, the picture was my first commission.

THE MOOR HEAD   C 1935

Sign of the Times

Very little remains today from this view of Moorhead around 1950. The Faie et Cie building, the Old Barleycorn public house, now a wine bar in Cambridge Street, and the City Hall (just visible) are still there.

The Crimea Monument was dismantled and the statue, later located in the Botanical Gardens, has now been put into storage. The column was taken down and used in a children's playground in Netherthorpe.

Townhead

The junction of Leopold Street and Church Street was the site of one of Sheffield's three crosses, namely, the Townhead Cross. On the left of the painting is the former Junior, and later the Central Technical School forming part of the Education Office block, which included the City Grammar School. Across the road, the more modern telephone building dominates the skyline, as the road winds its way up to West Street. The old town pinfold gave its name to Pinfold Street, now leading to Trippet Lane. The van on the left advertises Holmes and Younie, an old established motor company once operating from Suffolk Road.

Pinstone Street

This 1930s scene of the top section of Pinstone Street, leading into Town Hall Square and the Peace Gardens, shows trams loading passengers at the covered stop. A separate track allowed through trams to pass freely. The rear wall of the covered stop was the old St. Paul's church wall, removed when the Peace Gardens were further developed in recent years.

Hillsborough Corner

A United fan and a Wednesday fan discuss their clubs' fortunes in this scene of Hillsborough Corner. A horse and cart on our streets is a rare sight these days. Changes have also been made to the junction to accommodate the Supertram system.